SAVAGE, S 591.

Desert animals

This book is due for return on or before the date shown below.

20 JAN 2020

WITHDRAWN

HR HALLAM COMMUNITY
TECHNOLOGY COLLEGE
LIBRARY

INTRODUCTION

Deserts are the hottest, driest places on earth. Over thousands of years, rocks have been worn down into soil made up of tiny grains of sand. When people think of a desert, they think of a sea of sand stretching as far as the eye can see. While some deserts are like this, others contain mountains, plants and bushes. Some plants, including **cacti**, survive all year round, while others appear only after rainfall. Plants provide food, moisture and shelter to desert animals.

For much of the year there are no clouds in the sky to shield the ground from the hot sun. During the day, it is baking hot with temperatures of up to 50°C. There are no clouds to trap the sun's heat and the nights can be very cold. Strong winds may whip the sand into a sand storm, making it impossible to see more than 10 cm ahead. When rain eventually falls, it may form a raging torrent, carrying sand and rocks with it.

Some animals have adapted to the harsh desert conditions. Many avoid the sun's heat by sheltering in a **burrow** beneath the sand or in a cave where it is cooler. Desert animals are able to survive on a small amount of water and some never drink at all. Even so, their water supply is often under threat. On the edge of some deserts, farmers grow crops that are kept alive using water drawn from deep below the ground. This may use up the scarce water supply quicker than it is naturally replaced.

▲ The desert tortoise avoids the heat of the day by sheltering in its burrow.

This desert stretches into the distance like a never-ending sea of sand. ▶

▲ The Arabian oryx almost disappeared through over-hunting. It has been successfully bred in zoos and returned to its natural **habitat**.

MAMMALS

There are many different types of **mammals** that are adapted to life in the desert. Large **herbivore** mammals have hooves that help them to walk on soft sand. They get moisture by eating grass and other desert plants.

▲ A dromedary camel has long hair on its head, throat, neck and hump to protect it against sunburn.

Dromedary camel

The dromedary camel has a large hump on its back (bactrian camels have two humps). This hump is a store of fat that the camel lives off when no food is available. Even in the hottest weather, a dromedary camel can go without water for a week if there is enough grass to eat. A dromedary can drink up to 200 litres of water in one go. Desert people have made use of camels for transport for thousands of years. They feed them dates, grain and grass. Camels are sometimes known as 'ships of the desert' because of their use as transport and also because of their rolling walk.

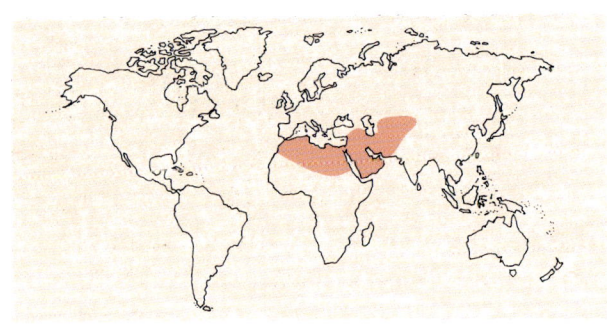

▲ The addax has a greyish-brown coat in the autumn that turns white in the summer to reflect the heat.

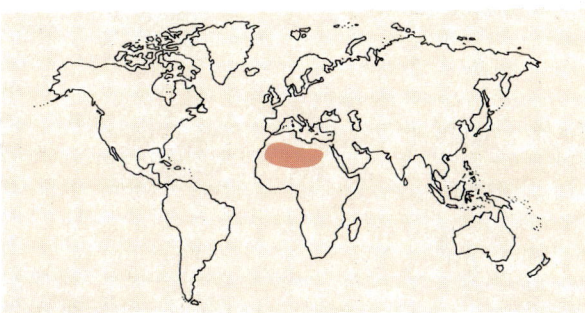

Addax

The addax is a large, heavy antelope. It lives in small herds and wanders through the desert looking for patches of grass to eat. The addax also feeds on the new leaves of desert plants that appear after seasonal rains. The addax gets water from grass and may never drink in its whole life. It is now nearly extinct in the wild due to hunting.

Arabian oryx

Like the addax, the Arabian oryx lives in small herds. It feeds mainly on clumps of grass found scattered across the desert. When they have eaten, the herd of oryx continues to travel, often in the cool hours of the night. The oryx gallops away if frightened. A herd usually runs together so that it is harder for a **predator** to single one oryx out. If cornered, an oryx will charge with its head down and attack the predator with its sharp horns.

▲ A herd of Arabian oryx travelling in search of food.

MAMMALS

Desert cats and foxes are perfectly adapted to life in or around the desert. They avoid the heat of the sun by sheltering in burrows and caves. Their sandy-coloured fur helps them to stalk their prey without being seen. Cats and foxes do not have to drink very often because they get most of the water they need from their food.

Fennec fox

The fennec fox is the smallest type of fox, growing no taller than 40 cm. It spends the day resting in its cool burrow and goes out to hunt at night. The fennec fox uses its large ears to listen for **prey** and danger. It eats insects, spiders and small mammals such as the jerboa. The female fox gives birth to her cubs and rears them in the safety of the burrow.

▲ The fennec fox keeps cool by getting rid of unwanted body heat through its large ear flaps.

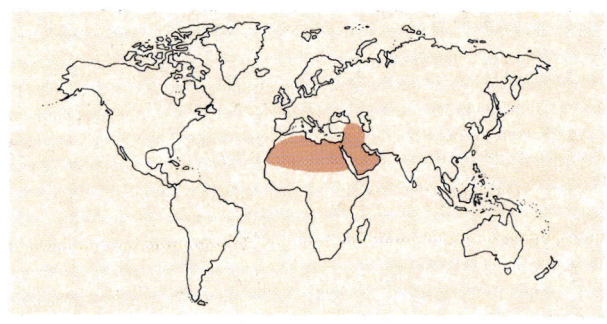

12

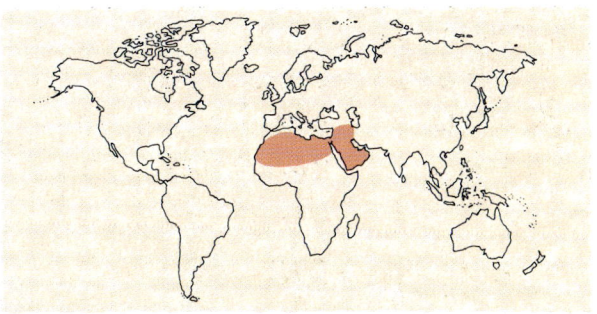

▲ The caracal's long legs are ideal for short bursts of speed.

Sand cat

The sand cat grows to a height of 60 cm and looks like a domestic cat. Its body fur is browny-yellow with black markings on its face, legs and tail. The sand cat is a **nocturnal** hunter that eats rodents, lizards and insects. It avoids the heat of the sun by sheltering in small caves during the day. Like many desert hunters, the undersides of the sand cat's feet have fur on them to help it walk in the soft sand.

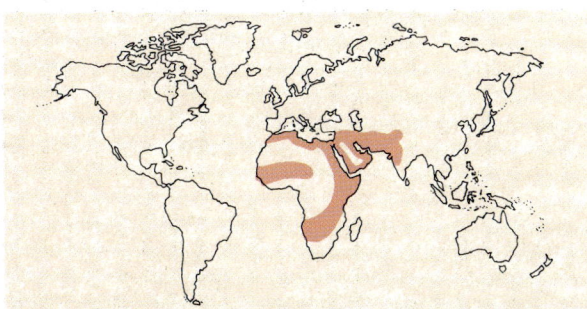

Caracal

When running over short distances, the caracal is one of the fastest cats in the world. It lives on the edge of the desert and sleeps during the day in caves, rocky **crevices** and abandoned burrows. As the sun sets and shadows fall across the desert, the caracal leaves its shelter to hunt. Birds are its favourite prey, particularly sand grouse. A caracal can leap up to 2 m into the air to catch an escaping bird. It also eats jerboas, small antelopes and lizards.

▲ The sand cat pounces on its prey just like a domestic cat.

MAMMALS

Many small mammals live in the desert, including several types of group-living jerboa and ground squirrel. Others, like the the unusual marsupial mole, live alone. The safest place for small mammals is beneath the sun-scorched sand.

Egyptian Jerboa

The Egyptian jerboa is one of several types of mouse-like rodents known as jerboas. These mammals hide from predators and the heat of the sun in underground burrows. Jerboas are nocturnal and leave the burrow at night to feed on seeds, leaves and insects. They get all the water they need from their food. Jerboas have excellent hearing and constantly listen for predators, including fennec foxes and snakes. If a snake enters its burrow, the jerboa escapes using an emergency exit. A small jerboa can take leaps of 1.5 m to escape from a predator.

▲ As the jerboa hops along the ground on its long back legs it looks like a miniature kangaroo.

14

Marsupial Mole

This mole belongs to a special group of mammals called **marsupials**. The young marsupial mole develops inside its mother's pouch just like a young kangaroo. The marsupial mole's body is covered in silky fur. It has large, flat claws for digging and hard skin to protect its nose as it burrows its head into the sand.

This shy, blind mole eats insects and lizards. ▼

▲ When danger is near, an antelope squirrel stands very still. Its white body stripe helps to disguise it from predators.

Antelope squirrel

The antelope squirrel is a type of ground squirrel that shelters from danger and predators in an underground burrow. It looks like a tree squirrel, but has shorter ears and legs and a less bushy tail. The young squirrels are born in a grass-lined den within the burrow, where they stay for six weeks. Unlike most small desert mammals, antelope squirrels are active during the day but they shelter to avoid the midday sun. The biggest danger to the young squirrels comes from rattlesnakes entering the burrow.

BIRDS

Deserts are rich in birdlife. Most birds have a higher body temperature than mammals and are better adapted to survive the heat of the desert. They are also able to fly very long distances in search of water.

Lanner falcon

The lanner falcon hunts birds, small mammals and lizards, including those that have come to drink at watering-holes. It gets all the moisture it needs from its food. It is the least powerful falcon, but the one best adapted to desert life. Gliding at a height of 500 m, the lanner falcon swoops down to attack its prey. It sometimes hunts in pairs – the female falcon flies low to disturb small birds which are then caught in mid-air by the male as they try to escape. Lanner falcons nest on the rocky ledges of desert cliffs.

◀ The lanner falcon grabs its prey with its large talons and eats using its strong beak.

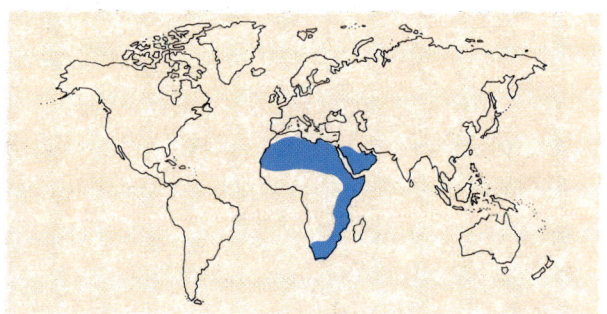

▲ Like all owls, the elf owl has large eyes for good vision.

Elf owl

At only 13 cm tall, the elf owl is one of the smallest owls in the world. It lives and nests in old woodpecker nest holes that have been made in large saguaro cacti. These tall cacti are covered with sharp, prickly thorns which help protect the nest hole. Elf owls rest during the day, safe and cool inside their nest. They come out at dusk to hunt for insects, spiders and lizards.

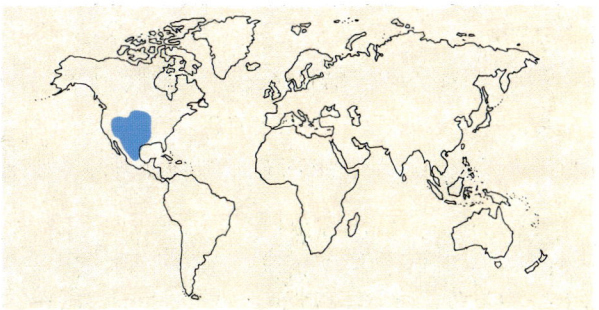

Burrowing owl

The burrowing owl grows to approximately 23 cm and has longer legs than most owls. Although capable of digging its own burrows, the burrowing owl prefers to use tunnels that have been left by other animals. A burrowing owl eats large insects, lizards and small mammals, especially those that have entered its burrow. If a predator tries to enter its burrow, the owl makes a noise like a rattlesnake to frighten it away.

Burrowing owls are day-active owls. ▶ They spend most of the day standing at the burrow entrance.

BIRDS

Some small birds, including the budgerigar, also manage to survive the harsh conditions of the desert. The roadrunner, made popular through cartoons, is another desert dweller.

Budgerigar

Budgerigars live in very large flocks. In times of drought, they migrate towards the coast and can sense when it is going to rain. Budgerigars get most of their water from seeds and can survive for up to six months without drinking. The young are fed on 'budgie milk', which is a special fluid that the mother produces and passes to her young through her beak. Budgerigars are able to fly at one month old.

▲ Budgerigars breed in large colonies. A male and female budgerigar often pair for life.

Roadrunner

The roadrunner can run at 40 kph which is very impressive for a bird the size of a chicken! When running, the roadrunner uses its short wings for balance and its large tail as a rudder. The roadrunner rarely flies. It avoids the midday sun by sheltering in the shade and hunts in the early morning, catching small mammals, birds, lizards, snakes and insects. Roadrunners' nests are often built in cactus plants and the prickly spines help protect the nests from predators.

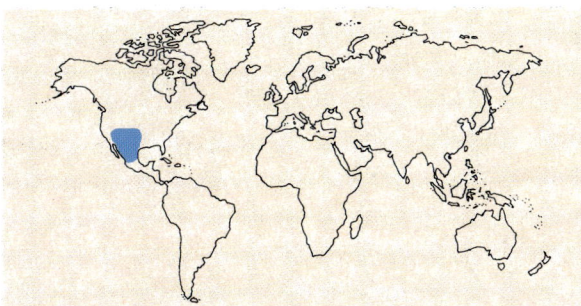

The bold, inquisitive roadrunner is a relative of the cuckoo. ▼

▲ The namaqua sand grouse has sand-coloured feathers that help camouflage it from desert predators.

Namaqua sand grouse

The namaqua sand grouse is a fast long-distance flyer. It flies great distances to find water every morning and evening and is able to drink dirty water when there is no clean water available. The namaqua sand grouse mainly eats seeds and so food is available all year round. While rearing chicks, the sand grouse fetches water for its young. The male grouse wades into water and its special feathers soak up the water like a sponge. It then flies back to its chicks, who suck the water from its soggy feathers.

REPTILES

Reptiles are **cold-blooded** animals, which means that their body temperature is controlled by the surrounding air temperature. Reptiles survive in the desert by warming their bodies in the sun's heat and sheltering when it becomes too hot. Lizards use various unusual methods to find food and water and to escape from predators.

▲ The gila monster has bright warning colours and can grow up to 45 cm long.

Gila monster

The gila monster is one of only two lizards that has a poisonous bite. It feeds on small mammals, birds and other lizards swallowed whole. It also eats birds' eggs, which it shatters before eating. Gila monsters sense their prey by using their tongue and a special organ in their mouth. Their fat tail is a food store which they live off in the dry season. Gila monsters lay their eggs in the sand and these hatch one month later.

▲ The web-footed gecko uses its excellent eyesight to spot the movement of its prey.

Thorny devil

The thorny devil lizard has sharp, spiny scales covering its body, legs and tail which are a good defence against most desert predators. During cold nights, **dew** collects on the large scales and passes down along special grooves into the lizard's mouth. The thorny devil grows up to 15 cm long and eats mainly ants.

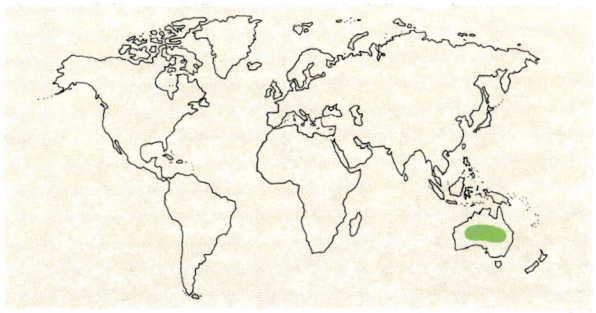

Web-footed gecko

The web-footed gecko is one of several types of gecko that live in the desert. It uses its webbed feet for digging and also to help stop it from sinking in the sand. The gecko lives in a burrow during the day and searches for insects at night. If attacked, the gecko can shed its tail – the attacker is left with the tail while the gecko escapes. In time the gecko will grow a new tail.

The fearsome-looking thorny devil is harmless to humans. ▼

REPTILES

There are many different types of desert snake, including the poisonous spitting cobra and the harmless milk snake. Snakes find their prey by flicking their tongue in and out, collecting scents on the tip of it. The various scents are transferred to sensory organs in the snake's mouth.

Desert king snake

Unlike the rattlesnake and the cobra, the desert king snake is not poisonous. It eats other snakes, sometimes over half its own size and even eats small and medium-sized rattlesnakes. The desert king snake kills its prey by wrapping its body around its victim and squeezing. It then swallows its meal whole!

▲ Although the desert king snake has black and yellow markings, it is not a poisonous snake.

Western diamondback rattlesnake

The diamondback rattlesnake is named after the segments on the tip of its tail, which vibrate when the tail is shaken. Like all reptiles, the rattlesnake sheds its skin as it grows. A new segment is added to its tail each time its skin is shed and so the rattle gets louder as the snake gets older. The rattlesnake has special pits on its face, between its nostrils and eyes. These act as a heat sensor to detect the body heat of its prey.

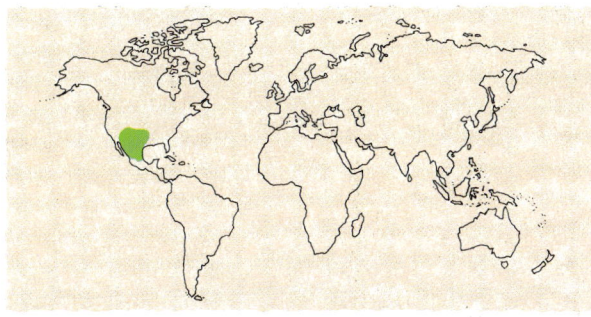

Rattlesnakes eat small mammals, but may themselves be eaten by other snakes, roadrunners and people. ▼

▲ The red cobra only spits poison at a would-be attacker as a last defence.

Red cobra

The red cobra lives by oases where prey is easier to find. It is a night hunter, feeding on small mammals, birds, toads and other reptiles, including snakes. When threatened, the cobra spreads out special skin around its neck to make a threatening hood. The snake also hisses and if approached, will spit **venom** into the eyes of its attacker. Like the rattlesnake, the red cobra bites its prey with two fangs which inject poison.

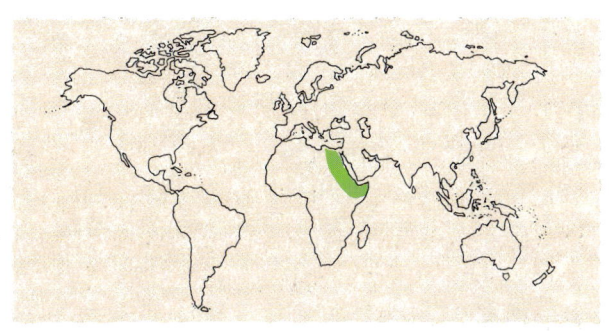

AMPHIBIANS

Amphibians are water-loving animals that we would usually expect to live in a damp habitat rather than a dry desert. However, some frogs and toads are cleverly adapted to life in a dry environment.

Green desert toad

The green desert toad lives by oases. It shelters under stones during the day and hunts for food at night. Green toads feed on insects that are attracted to the water at the oasis. They also hunt for insects amongst desert plants. The green desert toad lays its eggs in water. Because there is a constant supply of water at the oasis, the green toad does not have to speed up the development of its eggs and tadpoles to fit in with the short rainy season.

▲ Green desert toads have large poison glands on their heads which make them taste very unpleasant to predators.

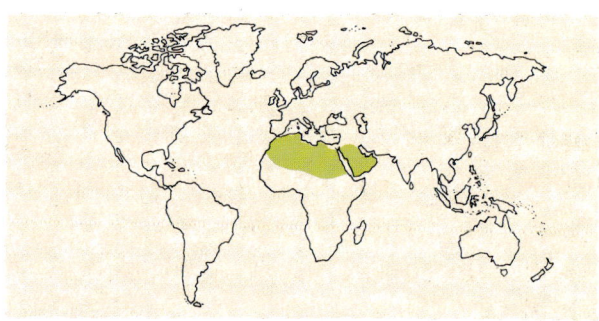

INDEX

Page numbers of illustrations are in bold.

amphibians 24–25
antelopes 11
  addax **11**
ant-lion 28, **29**
ants 21
  harvester **28**
  honey pot 28, **29**

birds 16–19
  budgerigar **18**
  burrowing owl **17**
  elf owl **17**
  lanner falcon **16**
  namaqua sand
    grouse **19**
  roadrunner 18, **19**
burrows 4, 12, 14,
  15, 17, 21, 25

cactus/cacti (plural)
  4, 9
  saguaro **9**, 17
camels
  bactrian 10
  dromedary **10**
camouflage 19
cats
  caracal **13**
  sand **13**

caves 4, 12, 13

foxes
  fennec **12**, 14
frogs
  water-holding **25**

geckos
  web-footed **21**

herbivores 10

insects 17, 19, 26
  jewel wasp **27**
  Namib darkling
    beetle **27**
invertebrates 26–29

lizards 13, 16, 17,
  19, 20
  gila monster **20**
  thorny devil **21**

mammals 10–15
  16, 19, 20, 23
marsupials
  moles 14, **15**

Namib Desert **7**

oasis/oases (plural)
  8, **9**, 23, 24
oryx
  Arabian **5, 11**

predators 11, 14,
  15, 17, 19, 20, 21,
  24, 26, 27, 28
prey 12, 13, 16, 23,
  26

reptiles 20–23
rodents 13
  antelope squirrel
    15
  Egyptian jerboa **14**

scorpions
  Sahara desert **26**
snakes 14, 15, 19
  desert king **22**
  milk 22
  rattle 15, 17, 22
  red cobra **23**
  western
    diamondback **23**
spiders 17, 26

toads
  green desert **24**
  spadefoot **25**
tortoises
  desert **4**

▲ Worker honey pot ants bring honey dew back to the nest to be stored inside the bodies of these repletes.

Ant-lion

Ant-lions are large desert insects that look similar to dragonflies. The ant-lion larva builds a funnel-shaped pit and hides beneath the sand at the bottom of the pit. The pit may be up to 5 cm deep and 8 cm wide. Any insects, particularly ants, that fall into the pit are grasped in the young ant-lion's jaws and eaten.

After its meal the ant-lion larva (left) buries itself back in the sand and lies in wait for more insects. ▼

Honey pot ants

Honey pot worker ants collect a sugary fluid called honey dew from aphids and cochineal insects. The worker ants stroke the aphids and insects with their antennae so that they produce a drop of honey dew. Special ants, called repletes, turn themselves into living 'honey pots'. Their swollen bodies become stores for the honey dew. These living honey pots cannot move so they hang from the roof of the nest. In the dry season, when food is scarce, the honey pot ants feed the rest of the ant community.

INVERTEBRATES

The harvest ant and the honey pot ant are two very different types of ant that live in the desert. Both types live in colonies in underground nests ruled by a single queen ant. Much of their time is spent collecting food and avoiding predators, such as the ant-lion.

▲ Worker harvester ants leave a scent trail so that they can find their way back to the nest.

Harvester ant

Worker harvester ants are female. They build the nest and collect food, travelling up to 100 m away to collect seeds. Worker ants are very strong and can carry seeds larger than themselves. The seeds are collected at the end of the wet season and stored as food for the dry season. Soldier harvester ants crack the seeds open with their strong jaws and the empty husks are left outside the nest entrance.

28

▲ The Namib darkling beetle is one of several dew-collecting beetles.

Namib darkling beetle

The Namib darkling beetle has a clever way of obtaining drinking water from sea fog. It stands with its head down and its abdomen pointing up in the air. Moisture collects on the beetle's abdomen and trickles down the underside of its body to its mouth. The Namib darkling beetle searches for food during the day and stays buried in the sand at night, except when there is a night fog. If attacked by a predator, it can defend itself by squirting poison from its abdomen.

Jewel wasp

The solitary jewel wasp takes great care providing for its young. When the female is ready to lay eggs it makes a nest in the sand. It hunts for a large insect and stings it. It then drags the insect inside its nest and lays an egg on the insect before sealing up the nest. The insect is paralysed but alive, and is food for the newly hatched larva. The female jewel wasp repeats this process for each egg. After two weeks the **larva** becomes an adult and feeds on plant nectar.

The jewel wasp is named after its shiny blue-green body. ▼

INVERTEBRATES

A variety of insects and other tiny creatures live in the desert. Like the larger desert animals, they face a difficult battle against the harsh conditions. Many have developed very unusual ways of catching food and collecting water.

Sahara desert scorpion

The Sahara desert scorpion is one of several scorpions found in deserts worldwide. It has an armoured body and a large sting on its tail. The sting can be used as a warning against predators or to sting struggling prey. Desert scorpions mainly eat insects and spiders and get all their water from their food. A scorpion will only attack a human if it feels threatened. Baby scorpions ride on their mother's back, underneath the safety of her sting, until they are old enough to survive on their own.

◀ The Sahara desert scorpion uses its large claws to catch prey.

▲ In the dry season, spadefoot toads live off their body fat and water stored in their bladders.

Spadefoot toad

As their name suggests, spadefoot toads have large spade-like feet for digging. They spend up to ten months of the year resting beneath the sand and only leave their burrows in the rainy season. The female lays her eggs, which hatch after two days, in rain-filled pools. The tadpoles mainly feed on **algae** and dead creatures, but when food is scarce they may eat each other. The tadpoles become adult frogs in two weeks. As the pools dry up, the frogs burrow under the sand and the cycle begins again.

Water-holding frog

Water-holding frogs spend much of their life underground and only leave their burrows in the rainy season. As the rain-filled pools begin to dry, they absorb water into their bodies and become round and bloated. They burrow under the sand and make a chamber where they can stay for at least two years. Water-holding frogs produce a special skin around their body that traps water underneath. **Aborigines** sometimes dig up these drogs and drink water from them.

The water-holding frog must make a new burrow before the ground dries up again. ▼